FINALLY CHOOSING MYSELF

DURGAM AJAY

*For everyone who forgot to choose themselves
first.
For the quiet hearts and tired souls who kept
going anyway.
And for the girl I still carry in my silence—
This is for you.*

*To Smiley,
you were more than just a chapter in my life.
You were the poetry in between the lines.
And even now—
you still teach me how to love myself*

— The boy who finally choose himself

Contents

Foreword

This book is not just a story—it's a piece of my heart wrapped in words, a silent scream turned into pages, and a journey that began in the soft glow of first love and wandered into the darkest corners of loss. Finally Choosing Myself is for anyone who's ever loved deeply, lost suddenly, and had to rebuild slowly.

It started with a boy named Nani and a girl named Smiley. Two hearts that found each other in the chaos of high school hallways, in stolen glances, in laughter that echoed longer than time itself. And then—life happened. The kind of life that changes everything in a heartbeat.

This is a story about love, but more than that, it's about grief. It's about how sometimes the people we lose take a part of us with them, and how it feels to live with that absence. It's about how the world keeps turning even when you want it to pause, just for a moment. And most importantly, it's about healing—not the kind that comes quickly, but the kind you have to fight for, every single day.

If you've ever felt like the pain might never end, if you've ever stood at the edge of your own breaking point, I want you to know you're not alone. I've been there. And somehow, through it all, I learned something powerful—sometimes the bravest thing you can do is choose yourself. Not just once, but over and over again.

So here it is. My truth. My story. My way of letting go, by holding on to what matters.

I hope these words help you feel seen.

With love,

—Durgam Ajay

Preface

This is not just a story.
It is a memory wrapped in moonlight,
a scar that still sings some nights,
a love that lived like fire—and ended like silence.

I never meant to write these pages.
But when your soul holds too much,
the words begin to pour out,
dripping from the cracks where your heart once bled.

There was a boy—bright-eyed, full of plans,
who fell in love with a girl
whose smile felt like home.
And just when life felt like it was beginning,
everything broke.

This book is not about perfection.
It is about pain.
It is about standing at the edge of everything you once believed in,
and somehow choosing not to jump.
It is about choosing to live,
even when the world feels like it's made of echoes and ashes.

And in the end, it is about the quiet, powerful decision to stop waiting to be saved—
and save yourself.

So if you're here,
if you're reading this,
thank you.

I hope you find pieces of your own heart in these words.
I hope they make you feel seen.

Acknowledgements

To those who held me when I couldn't hold myself—
thank you.
To the ones who saw my silence and stayed anyway,
who never rushed my healing or tried to fix what was
meant to be felt—
this book carries your quiet love in every line.
To my friends who listened to the same stories over and
over,
as if they were brand new each time—
you never knew how much that meant.
You helped me breathe when it felt like I couldn't.
To my family—thank you for giving me the space to fall
apart
and the strength to rebuild.
To the readers—
whether you came for the story, the sadness, the hope, or
the healing—
thank you for making space in your heart for mine.
To Smiley—
you were the spark, the ache, the muse.
You changed everything.
This book is a love letter to what we had,
and a goodbye I never got to say.
And finally,
to the version of me that kept going
when every part wanted to give up—
I'm proud of you.
You made it.
You chose yourself.
And that is where the healing began.

Prologue

Maybe the journey isn't about becoming anything.
Maybe it's about unbecoming everything that isn't truly you,
so you can finally be who you were meant to be."

-Durgam Ajay

CHAPTER ONE

Nani - The Merit Boy

It was the beginning of yet another academic year. For most students, it meant dragging themselves back into routine—but for Nani, it was another step toward excellence.

Nani wasn't just any student. He was the kind who sat in the first bench, answered every question with clarity, and never missed a single assignment. Teachers admired him, classmates respected him, and his parents saw him as their proudest achievement. Quiet, disciplined, and always immersed in books, Nani lived a life with one simple rule—study hard, succeed, and make no mistakes.

His world was small. Home, school, and his books were the three pillars of his existence. He had a few friends, but he never let anyone too close. Emotions were distractions, he believed. Love was something for movies—not for someone with goals like his.

But fate doesn't knock. It walks right in—often wearing a smile.

It was the second week of school. The morning assembly had just ended when Nani noticed a girl standing quietly near the principal's office. She was new—uniform perfectly pressed, two braids hanging neatly on either side, and a face that somehow seemed to be smiling even when she wasn't.

He didn't know it then, but that moment would be carved in his memory forever.

Later that day, their teacher introduced her to the class.

"This is Smiley. She's joined us from Vizag. Please make her feel welcome."

She gave a soft smile and a slight nod. When her eyes met Nani's, something unusual happened—he didn't look away.

" ✉? [A diary entry – a few weeks later]
Date: 12th July 2019
Dear Diary,
I don't know what's happening to me. I still top the tests, still finish my homework, but when she walks into the classroom… I forget formulas.
Her name is Smiley. What kind of name is that? But it fits. She laughs with her whole face, even her eyes smile.
Is this a crush? Or am I just losing focus? I can't tell…
- Nani"

Weeks passed. Smiley wasn't like other girls. She wasn't the loudest, nor the most popular, but she had a way of making even silence feel warm. They got paired for a science project, and that was the beginning.

They began texting. A few simple hellos turned into long, late-night chats. She once sent him a voice note laughing at her own silly joke. He played it five times.

And slowly, the boy who believed emotions were distractions… was falling.

"? A poem from Nani's notebook (unshared)
"The Girl Who Smiled in Silence"
I built walls of books and bricks,
Chased dreams with sharpened tricks,
But then she came—a quiet breeze,
With eyes that laughed and heart at ease.
She didn't speak in grand display,
Just smiled and took the clouds away.
And in that silence, I found a place,
A rhythm, a reason, a softer pace.
The days that followed were different."

Nani, who once lived by a strict timetable, now found himself waiting—not for a new chapter in his textbook, but for Smiley's messages. A "hi" from her made his whole day better. The sound of her laughter in the corridor gave him butterflies he didn't even know existed.

They sat together in class whenever possible. She'd pass little doodles to him on paper—tiny suns with sunglasses, or a panda reading a book labeled "Nani's Brain." He'd pretend to be annoyed, but secretly kept every note safe in a tin box at home.

One rainy afternoon, as they stood under the same umbrella outside the school gate, Smiley suddenly looked at him and said:

"You're weird, you know that?"
Nani raised an eyebrow. "Why?"
"Because you look serious all the time. But your eyes tell a different story."

That was the first time someone saw past his walls.

"⊠? [Diary Entry – August 4ᵗʰ, 2019]
Dear Diary,

She's like monsoon rain. Unexpected, soft, but powerful enough to shift everything.
I didn't know a girl could make me feel seen. Not like a topper. Not like a role model. Just... me.
When she talks, time doesn't just slow down—it listens.
God, am I falling in love?"

CHAPTER TWO

Smiley - The New Girl

Smiley had a way of walking into a room and changing the air without even trying. She wasn't loud, but people noticed her. Not for what she said—but for the way she made them feel.

She noticed Nani, too—long before he realized it.

To everyone else, he was "the topper." Always serious, never missing a beat. But to Smiley, he looked like someone who hadn't been hugged in a long time. She liked the way his eyes squinted slightly when he focused. The way he paused before answering a question, like he was measuring every word carefully.

They grew close. Fast. Naturally.

Lunch breaks became their quiet time. Nani would open his tiffin box, and Smiley would steal the aloo fry with a grin. They spoke about everything—from physics problems to how annoying group projects were. But there were things Smiley never said out loud.

"✉? [Unsent Letter – Written in her journal]
To the boy who doesn't know he saved me,
*   You probably think you're just another nerd with*
a goal chart on your wall. But you're more than that.

When I first came here, I felt like a stranger in my own skin. New city, new school, same old loneliness. I thought I'd float through this year like a ghost.

But then, you.

Your silence felt familiar. Like mine. And when you smiled—God, Nani, it felt like maybe I wasn't invisible anymore.

I don't know if this is love. Or just the first time I've felt safe in someone's presence. But whatever it is... thank you.

- Smiley ?

(never sent)"

One evening, as they walked around the school ground after class, Smiley stopped and looked up at the sky.

"Do you believe in soulmates?" she asked.

Nani blinked. "Soulmates? I'm still trying to believe in the periodic table."

She laughed—that laugh—and lightly nudged his arm. "I think I met mine," she whispered, mostly to herself.

Nani didn't reply. But in that moment, he knew.

CHAPTER THREE

The Connection

It wasn't planned. Love never is.

It happened on a Wednesday after school. The corridor was almost empty, except for a few kids hanging around. Nani was standing near the library entrance, waiting for Smiley, fidgeting with the corner of his bag strap.

When she finally walked up, her face was glowing. Not from makeup or light, but from something else. Maybe peace. Maybe joy.

"You okay?" he asked.

She nodded. Then paused. Then tilted her head.

"Nani... do you like me?" she asked, like she was asking if he liked mangoes—casual, soft, deadly.

He froze.

Then gave a slow, almost shy smile.

"Yes. I think I do."

She bit her lip. "Good. Because I think I like you too."

That was it. No big speech. No flowers. Just two teenagers standing in the hallway of a government school, hearts pounding like drums in a parade.

From that day, everything changed.

They didn't call it a relationship. They didn't need to. The way they looked at each other in class, the way they shared food, the way she rested her head on his shoulder during the bus ride home—it was all understood.

"? Poem from Smiley's Journal
"In the Space Between Us"
In the silence between your words,
I hear every heartbeat.
In the seconds our fingers touch,
The world forgets to speak.
We never wrote our names in trees,
Or shouted under stars,
But still—
You feel like poetry,
Soft-spoken and ours."

Sometimes they'd sneak to the terrace of the school after lunch, watching the sky change shades. Other times, they'd sit on calls until 1 a.m., listening to each other breathe when words ran out.

Smiley would tell him stories—some real, some made up. Nani would share little facts from his books just to hear her say, "You're such a nerd."

They were just two kids in love, with no idea that life was about to split them apart.

? Scene: After School – Rain and Chai

It was a cloudy Friday, and the first drizzle of the season had just started. Nani and Smiley stood under the tin roof near the school gate, waiting for the rain to calm down.

"Ever tried hot chai in this weather?" Smiley asked.

Nani shook his head. "I don't really go out much."

She grabbed his wrist and pulled him toward the small tea stall across the road.

They stood under one umbrella, steam from the cups mixing with the scent of wet soil. She took a sip, closed her eyes.

"Best feeling in the world," she said.

He watched her, more than the rain.

"You know what's better than chai?" he whispered.

She raised her eyebrows.

"This moment."

"? Unsent Letter from Smiley – Kept in her diary
Dear Nani,

There wasn't a specific day I fell in love with you. It happened slowly. Like tea cooling down, like paper soaking in ink.

Maybe it was the day you stayed silent when I cried about my mom yelling at me. You didn't say "it's okay." You just listened. And that was enough.

Or maybe it was when you shared your favorite pen with me—even though you treat your pens like museum pieces.

Or maybe... maybe I just always loved you. Even before I knew what that meant.

If you ever read this:
Yes, it was always you.
- Smiley ?

? Transcript – Nani's Late-Night Voice Message
Time: 12:46 AM
Sent on: November 18th, 2019

"Hey... you asleep?

Sorry—I know it's late. I just... I miss your voice. It's stupid, we just talked three hours ago.

I was trying to revise math, but your laugh kept echoing in my head instead of equations.

You're trouble, you know that?
Okay, go sleep. Goodnight, Smiley.
I think I'm falling—
[message ends abruptly]"
"

CHAPTER FOUR

Young Love

For eight months, the world didn't need to know what they were.

Because to them, it was already everything.

They had their little world—tucked inside science notes, secret glances across the classroom, and long walks down quiet streets. They didn't care about labels. What they had was something only they could understand.

Smiley started calling him "Professor Panda"—partly because of his brain, partly because of the way he squinted when reading.

Nani called her "Sunshine"—because she was the only one who could make a boring Monday feel like a festival.

? Scene: Shared Notebook – Smiley & Nani's Mini Journal
One day, Smiley gave Nani a small diary. "We'll pass it back and forth. Write anything. No rules."

They started writing random thoughts in it during class breaks.

Smiley's Page:
I wonder if I'll remember the way you look at me when I'm old and wrinkled.
I hope I do. It's the only mirror that makes me feel beautiful.
Nani's Page:

You're the reason I stopped seeing love as a distraction. Now it feels like a destination.

They made up stories together about classmates, wrote fake horoscopes, even planned a pretend trip to Goa "after boards." None of it mattered. What mattered was that they were writing a story together, one laugh at a time.

? Scene: Their First "I Love You"
It was the evening before Smiley's birthday. Nani had stayed up all night making her a hand-written card with tiny doodles of all their inside jokes.

He gave it to her in the school library, both pretending they were just studying.

She read it quietly, then looked up.
"I love you, Nani."

No hesitation. No big drama. Just pure, quiet truth.

He didn't speak for a moment. His throat felt dry. Then he reached over the table, touched her hand gently, and said,
"I love you too, Smiley. I think I've loved you for a long time. I just didn't know the word for it."

They weren't perfect. They had arguments—about silly things, like whether paneer or pizza was better. But even the fights ended with a smile and a "don't ever stop talking to me."

They thought they had forever.

"? Ending Note: From Nani's Future Diary
If I could go back to any day in my life, it wouldn't be a festival or a trip... it would be one of those simple days.
Where we laughed about nothing. Walked in the sun. Wrote to each other in the margins of math books.

I didn't know those were the golden hours of my life.
Until they were gone. "

? Memory: The Day of the Yellow Flower

It was a lazy Saturday in February. The school had declared a half-day for a teacher's meeting, and Nani and Smiley decided to walk home together—no uniforms, no backpacks, just themselves and a whole afternoon.

On their way, they passed a small park filled with blooming flowers. Children were playing, a few old men sat on benches reading newspapers, and the air smelled of roasted peanuts from a nearby stall.

Smiley suddenly stopped and pointed.

"Wait here," she said, and ran into the grass.

Nani watched as she bent down and picked a small yellow flower—half bloomed, almost shy like her smile.

She came back and tucked it behind his ear.

"There," she said, admiring her work. "Now you're perfect."

Nani blushed so hard he almost forgot how to breathe.

"You're crazy," he mumbled.

Smiley grinned. "Crazy enough to love you like this forever."

He didn't reply. He didn't need to. He just looked at her—the girl who ran through parks, who believed yellow flowers could fix broken days—and he smiled the kind of smile only she could pull out of him.

Later that night, she messaged him:

"Keep that flower safe, okay?

One day you'll need a piece of sunshine."

He pressed it in his notebook, between the pages of their shared journal.

Years later, it would still be there—dried, delicate, and unforgettable.

CHAPTER FIVE

March 2020 – Lockdown Begins

It started with whispers.

People talked about a virus in China, about some school in Delhi shutting down for "safety." Nani didn't think much of it—until his school declared holidays "until further notice."

Smiley looked at him that day with a strange sadness.

"Do you think it's serious?" she asked.

He shrugged. "A few weeks, max. It'll blow over."

He was wrong.

? First Few Weeks – All Online

At first, the lockdown felt like a mini vacation. No uniforms, no morning alarms. Just texts, memes, and voice calls. Nani and Smiley spent hours talking—about everything and nothing.

They'd play Ludo King together. Send each other Spotify playlists. Try video calling but always laugh awkwardly after the first five seconds.

They both missed the school canteen samosas.
They both missed each other.

"? Chat Transcript – April 6th, 2020
Smiley: ugh I miss your handwriting
Nani: why?
Smiley: because even your alphabets look like
they're trying too hard ?
Nani: rude
Smiley: real
Nani: I miss you
Smiley: I miss you too
Smiley: like... a lot.
Nani: we'll be okay right?
Smiley: of course. we're us. "

But as weeks turned into months, things began to shift.

Smiley started replying slower. Her texts became shorter. Sometimes she'd vanish for a day and say her Wi-Fi was acting up.

Nani didn't want to overthink it. Maybe she was just tired. Everyone was feeling weird. Trapped. But his heart... it noticed.

One night, after a long silence, she finally replied:

"I'm just feeling low lately. I don't know why. Sorry if I'm boring these days."

He replied instantly:

"You're not boring. You're my favorite person. Even when you're quiet."

She sent a red heart. But deep down, something in her tone had changed.

"⊠? Diary Entry – May 2020, Nani
Dear Diary,
I miss her voice. I miss her eyes.
I miss the way she always touched her braid when

she was nervous.
The chats are still there, the calls still happen, but it
feels like I'm holding a shadow of something real.
I'm scared. But I won't show it.
She needs me to be the strong one.
- Nani"

The world was crumbling outside. And inside their hearts, a quiet storm was beginning.

The Distance Between Us

The messages became more spaced out.

The calls shorter.

The laughter less frequent.

Nani tried to understand. He kept telling himself it was the lockdown. Everyone was exhausted. Maybe Smiley just needed time.

But sometimes, silence is louder than any goodbye.

> "? *Chat Transcript – June 3rd, 2020*
> *Nani: hey*
> *Smiley: hey*
> *Nani: how was your day?*
> *Smiley: okay. yours?*
> *Nani: boring. same. I miss seeing you*
> *Smiley: :)*
> *Nani: can we call tonight?*
> *Smiley: not today. head hurts.*
> *Nani: okay. feel better.*
> *Smiley: thanks. gn."*

He stared at that "gn" for hours that night, wondering where the warmth went.

? Smiley's Side – Her Silent Struggle

Smiley didn't know how to explain it.

She was trapped in a house that didn't feel like home, in a mind that didn't feel safe. Her parents were fighting more. Her grades had dropped. And a cold, nameless sadness had started sitting on her chest every morning.

Even texting Nani started to feel like lying.

Because she didn't want to tell him that sometimes she cried for no reason. That she couldn't concentrate. That she felt like a burden.

So instead... she sent emojis.

Pretended.

Withdrew.

> "? Poem – From Smiley's Journal
> "I Am Here, But Not"
> I smile with my fingers,
> Lie with my eyes.
> Tell everyone "I'm fine,"
> While a piece of me dies.
>   I wish I could scream,
> But I don't want to scare.
> So I sit with my silence—
> Pretending I'm there."

Nani started writing to her like he used to—sending old poems, memories, even jokes. But the replies were slower. Shorter. Sometimes, they didn't come at all.

He never stopped trying.

But she was already slipping away.

"? Diary Entry – Nani, July 2020
I don't know how to reach her anymore.
It's like I'm knocking on a door that used to be open.
Now it's locked, but I can hear her crying on the other side.
I'd wait forever if it meant she'd come back. But I'm scared I'll lose her before she even realizes she's gone.
"

CHAPTER SEVEN

Our Birthdays

? Smiley's Birthday – July 31, 2020

It was the quietest birthday she'd ever had. No friends over. No cake cutting in class. Just a few dry wishes from relatives and a reused party hat her mom found in the cupboard.

But then, at 12:01 a.m., her phone pinged.

From Nani:

"Check your mail ??"

He had written her a full digital letter titled:

"31 Reasons Why You're My Sunshine"

Some reasons were silly.

Like:

"#6 – You once asked if ducks have feelings. That melted me."

Some were beautiful.

"#17 – When you laugh at my worst jokes, I feel like the funniest guy alive."

And the last one:

"#31 – Because even when the world is dark, you still glow. And I never want to lose that light."

She cried reading it.

That morning, she messaged him:

"You gave me more than a party ever could. Thank you for reminding me I exist."

Later that day, she sent him a voice note:

"Nani... I love you more than I've ever said. Just... know that."

? Nani's Birthday – September 27, 2020

She remembered.

Even though things had become quiet, even though she barely smiled anymore—she remembered.

At midnight, he got a message with a short video.
It was Smiley's voice, shaky but warm.

"Happy birthday, my favorite boy."
"I know things aren't the same, but if I could, I'd teleport and bring you hot chocolate, a handmade card, and the biggest hug ever."
"Thank you for being the best part of my world."

He didn't get many gifts that year. But that message?
He replayed it 78 times.

Later that night, she sent one final message:

"I hope you always remember how loved you are, Nani. Even if I'm not around someday... never forget it."

At the time, he didn't think too much about that last line.
Now, it plays in his head like a warning he didn't hear in time.

The Last Message

It was a normal day.

That's what hurt the most.

There were no signs. No warning bells. No dramatic goodbye.

Smiley hadn't messaged in two days. Nani figured she was just caught up with online classes or feeling low again. He didn't want to pressure her. He thought giving her space was love.

Until 5:42 p.m. on a cloudy Wednesday, his phone buzzed.

"*? Smiley – Last Message*
"Nani... I don't think I can do this much longer."
"Please don't blame yourself. You gave me more love than I thought I deserved."
"I'm just tired. Tired in ways I can't explain."
"Thank you for making me feel like I mattered. You were the only real thing in my life."
"Please smile again someday. Don't let my darkness dim your light."
"I love you. I'm sorry.""

Nani didn't understand at first. He thought maybe she was overwhelmed again. Maybe she was just venting. Maybe she'd call after dinner and say, "Sorry, I freaked out."

But the call never came.

No more messages.

Just silence.

The next day, Smiley's number was unreachable. Her profile picture disappeared. Her mom wouldn't answer the phone.

Nani's hands trembled as he searched her name online.

One article.

Three lines.

A headline that shattered his soul.

"16-Year-Old Girl Found Dead in Suspected Suicide."
"Sources say she had been dealing with mental stress during the lockdown."

He dropped his phone.

Everything blurred.

Everything broke.

"? Diary Entry – Nani, October 2020

She didn't say goodbye.

She left pieces of herself in my poems, my notebooks, my heart—but not a proper goodbye.

Maybe she thought I'd be better off. Maybe she didn't want to see me cry.

But God, Smiley... I would've held your pain with both hands.

I would've stayed on the phone until sunrise. I would've told you again and again that you were enough.

Now all I have is silence.

And a message I'll never stop rereading.

"

CHAPTER NINE

The Aftermath

For the first month, Nani barely spoke.

He kept rereading her last message, hoping it would change.

Hoping maybe it was a mistake. A bad dream.

But the truth stayed.

His sunshine was gone.

? The World Without Her

Days blurred into nights. Nani stopped attending online classes. His smile vanished. Friends texted, then gave up. Teachers assumed he was just being lazy.

No one really knew.

No one really asked.

He avoided places they once shared—muted their old song, deleted Ludo King, skipped his birthday the next year entirely. He couldn't even write in his journal. Words felt too heavy.

But what hurt most... was the "what ifs."

What if I had called more?

What if I had asked harder?

What if I had said, "Don't go," louder?

"? *Unsent Letter – Nani to Smiley (2021)*
Dear Smiley,

I don't know if souls can read letters.
But if you can, I hope this reaches you.

I hope you're somewhere peaceful, where your thoughts don't hurt, and the sky is always your favorite shade of blue.

I wish I could've taken some of your pain. Just a little. Just enough for you to stay.

Sometimes, I close my eyes and pretend you're still here. Not in the past tense. Not as a memory. But here—messy braid, half-smile, stealing my fries.

I miss you every day.
But I'm trying.
Trying to keep the promise I never got to say out loud:

To smile again.

Love,
Nani"

? Years Pass
The pain never really left. But it changed.

In college, he started writing again. Quietly. At night. He joined a mental health club. He even shared Smiley's story once—voice shaking, but steady by the end.

Her photo stayed in his drawer.
The yellow flower stayed in his notebook.
And her voice? It lived in every poem he wrote.

He didn't move on.
He moved forward. With her in his shadow, his ink, his breath.

Now: Nani is older.
Stronger.
And for the first time in five years, he feels ready to share their story with the world.

To honor her.
To heal others.
To finally say goodbye in the way he never got to

CHAPTER TEN

Healing In The Hollow

Grief is not something you "get over."
It's something you grow around.

? First Year of College – 2023

By now, it had been almost three years since Smiley left. Nani had moved cities for college. New people. New room. New world.

But every night, before sleeping, he still whispered her name.

He kept a small photo of her tucked in the first page of his diary. He never told his roommates. He didn't need to.

Healing wasn't loud. It came in moments.

The first time he laughed without guilt.

The first time he heard a love song and didn't turn it off.

The first time he wrote "Smiley" in a poem and didn't cry.

"?? Excerpt from his poem – "I Didn't Forget You"
I didn't move on.
I just learned to live
with your echo in the quiet.
I still walk through your memory
but now, I leave the windows open."

? Therapy, Finally

In his second year, Nani started therapy.

Not because someone forced him—because one night he broke down after seeing someone with her smile, and he realized:

"I don't want to survive anymore. I want to live."

His therapist never rushed him.

She listened.

She said, "You don't have to let go of her to move forward."

That sentence became a turning point.

? A Chance Encounter

At a college open mic, Nani read a poem about grief. About a girl who loved sunflowers. About a boy still learning how to breathe without her.

After he finished, a girl from the crowd walked up to him and said:

"That was the most honest thing I've heard in years. Whoever she was, she must've loved you a lot."

Nani smiled. For the first time in forever, it didn't hurt to hear her name.

It felt... like honor.

? The Book Begins

One evening, staring at a blank document, Nani typed:

"This is the story of a boy who loved a girl named Smiley. She made him laugh, gave him poems, and then—left the world too soon. This is not a tragedy. This is a love letter."

That was the beginning.

The start of the book you're holding now.

A promise kept.

A voice returned.

A smile that would live on.

CHAPTER ELEVEN

Letters She'll Never Read

Some things can't be said out loud.
So Nani wrote them.
On napkins, in diaries, on the backs of receipts.
Every time he missed her too much—he wrote.

"?? July 31, 2021 – Smiley's Birthday
Dear Smiley,

Happy Birthday.
I would've given you 17 sunflowers today. One for every year you should've been alive.

I baked a cake. Just a small one. Vanilla. Your favorite.
I didn't light a candle. I just sat beside it and whispered stories to the walls.

I wonder what you'd have worn today. That pink hoodie? Or maybe that sunflower print dress you always said was "too much" but secretly loved.

I hope you're surrounded by light, wherever you are.
I hope your soul is warm.

And I hope, somehow, you still feel loved.

Love always,
Nani"

"*?? September 27, 2022 – His Own Birthday*
Hey Smiley,
Today's my birthday.
And the only gift I wanted... was your voice.
I tried to imagine what you'd have said.
Maybe: "Happy birthday, old man!" or "You're still
my favorite 9th class nerd."
Everyone thinks I've moved on.
Truth? I've just learned how to carry you quieter.
But I still miss you.
Not in a crying-every-night way. More like—missing
the warmth of sunlight on a rainy day.
I hope you'd be proud of me.
I'm trying, Smiley.
I swear, I'm trying.
Yours forever,
Nani"

"*?? Random Night – 3:11 A.M.*
Dear You,
Tonight, I couldn't sleep.
So I closed my eyes and walked into our imaginary
café again.
The one with rain outside and hot chocolate on the
table.
You were there. Smiling like before.
You reached out, touched my hand, and said,
"You're doing okay."
I believed you.

Please keep visiting me in dreams.
They're all I have left.
Nani
These letters were never mailed.
But they healed him.
Little by little.
Word by word.
Tear by tear.
"

CHAPTER TWELVE

The Day I Smiled Without Crying

It was nothing big.

No dramatic sunrise.

No deep quote on a wall.

Just a normal Tuesday.

Nani was walking back from college. Headphones in, random playlist on shuffle. His brain tired from back-to-back lectures. The sky was that soft, golden kind that Smiley used to say looked like a "painting from God."

Then a song came on.

Their song.

He paused, thumb hovering over the skip button.

His usual reflex.

But this time...

He didn't skip.

He let it play.

And for the first time in years, as the music swirled through his ears and her memory danced through his heart—

He smiled.

No tears.

No chest ache.

Just a quiet, full smile.
Because in that moment, she wasn't gone.
She was with him.
In the wind.
In the lyrics.
In the golden sky.
And it didn't hurt.

"? Diary Entry – That Night
"I think today was the first day I smiled for real."
"I didn't cry. I didn't break. I just... remembered her
in peace."
"Maybe this is healing.""

The grief didn't disappear after that.
But now, Nani knew: he could carry it and still keep going.
He could live.
He could love again someday.
And she'd always be a part of him—not as a wound, but as a
chapter that made him who he is.

CHAPTER THIRTEEN

Sunflowers Still Bloom

Healing doesn't arrive like thunder.
It grows—like a sunflower in a crack of concrete.
Slow. Quiet. But real.

? The Small Garden Behind the College
It started as a way to escape stress. A patch of dirt behind
the college . No one really used it.

One weekend, Nani picked up some soil, cleared weeds,
and planted four seeds.

Sunflower seeds.

He didn't tell anyone what they meant.
But he watered them every morning.
Said her name while doing it—softly, like a prayer.

Weeks passed. One sprouted. Then two.

And when the first bright yellow flower opened its face
to the sun—
Nani sat beside it, smiling.

"You still bloom," he whispered.
"So I will too."

? New Friendships, Old Soul
He wasn't the loudest guy in his class.
But people noticed him more now.
Not because of his pain—but because of his kindness.

He listened when others vented.
He smiled even on tired days.
He checked on people quietly, like he wished someone had done for her.

That's how healing worked—it turned pain into empathy.

And slowly, the universe began sending people into his life who got it.

Not to replace Smiley.

But to remind him: he still belongs here.

"? Poem from His Notebook – "For the Ones Who Left Too Early"
You are not forgotten.
You are not a ghost.
You are sun in my memory,
rain in my rest,
and poems in my pulse.
I walk forward,
not away—
but with you in my stride.
In the cracks of sadness, joy started growing again.
Not the same joy.
But a new kind. Wiser. Softer.
Rooted in everything he lost, and everything he still had."

CHAPTER FOURTEEN

The Book I Promised You

It began with a single sentence:

"This is the story of a boy who loved a girl named Smiley."

Nani typed it one rainy evening, seated by the window with a cup of chai, her favorite.

No fancy writing space. No plan. Just his heart and the ache that wouldn't leave.

✍? Why He Wrote

He didn't write to "move on."

He wrote to keep her alive.

To give their love a place to breathe.

To remember the 8 months of magic, not just the day of loss.

To turn pain into something that could help someone else not feel alone.

And more than anything—

He wrote because he promised her.

In a voice note she once sent, she said:

"You'll be a great writer one day, Nani. And when you do, just don't forget to mention me somewhere... okay?"

This book?
It was that mention.

> "*? Excerpt – Early Draft*
> *"We were just kids when we fell in love. I was a topper. She was chaos in a hoodie. But when she laughed, the world felt okay."*
>
> *"We didn't last forever. But we lasted long enough to change me."*

?? The Cover Design
He doodled dozens of ideas. But finally, he picked a simple one:
A sunflower in the corner.
A half-scribbled poem across the center.
And the title she would've loved:
"Love in the Time of Lockdown"
He imagined her holding it.
Laughing at the title.
Correcting his grammar.

> "*⌧? Final Unsent Letter – Nani to Smiley*
> *Smiley,*
> *This is your book.*
> *Every sentence has your shadow.*
> *Every chapter is a piece of us.*
> *I don't know who will read it.*
> *But if it saves even one heart, makes one lonely soul feel seen—*
> *then I've done my job.*
> *Thank you for giving me a love worth writing about.*

> *Always yours,*
> *Nani*”

And with that, the book begins.
The real one.
The one you, dear reader, are holding now.
   It's not just a story of heartbreak.
It's a story of memory, music, poetry, pain, and soft healing.
   Of Nani and Smiley.
Of two hearts that met too early... and stayed forever.

CHAPTER FIFTEEN

Her Birthdays Without Her

July 31.

Every year, it came like a wave.

Her birthday.

Smiley's day.

The first year, Nani didn't leave his bed.

The second year, he cried into a poem and ripped it apart.

But this year—her third birthday without her—he decided to do something different.

? The Celebration She Deserved

He bought 17 yellow balloons. One for each year she would've been.

He picked a quiet spot in the city park—a bench under a gulmohar tree.

Brought cupcakes. Vanilla, like she loved.

And he sat.

Not alone.

This time, he invited three friends who knew bits of her through his stories.

They didn't try to cheer him up.

They just listened.

Let him talk.

Let him smile.

"*She used to hum songs without knowing the lyrics.*"
"*She hated physics but loved the stars.*"
"*She said my handwriting looked like it was running away from the page.*"
"*She once made me a paper ring. I still have it.*"

And then, quietly, he stood...
And released the 17 balloons into the evening sky.

"*? Birthday Poem – "Seventeen Skies"*
I sent you seventeen skies tonight,
Each one wrapped in a wish:
That you're laughing,
That you're dancing,
That you're free.
That somewhere,
Somehow,
You felt me remembering."

? A Playlist Called "July 31"
Later that night, Nani made a playlist.
Ten songs. All songs she used to love.
He didn't cry this time. He just listened.
Eyes closed. Head leaned back. Heart full.

For the first time, her birthday didn't break him.
It brought her back.

Not as a ghost.
But as joy.

Smiley may not age anymore.
But her memory grows.
With every year. Every page. Every smile Nani gives to someone else.

CHAPTER SIXTEEN

Love Doesn't End Here

It's been nearly five years now.
Five birthdays without her.
Five monsoons.
Five long walks home with her memory riding shotgun.
 Nani is still studying—second year of college.
Still learning, not just formulas or dates, but how to live with loss.
How to breathe without her name hurting his chest.

"? *Grief Isn't a Line. It's a Loop.*
Some mornings still sting.
Sometimes, he still picks up his phone and forgets she won't reply.
But now, he smiles at the ache.
Because it means she mattered.
 And you don't "move on" from that.
You move forward."

? What He's Built from Pain
A sunflower patch in the corner of campus.

A notebook full of poems that classmates borrow to cry into.
A soft heart that others trust.
A book—this book—the promise he kept.
And most of all:
A version of himself that Smiley would've been proud of.

"? If She Could Read This, He'd Say:
"Thank you for teaching me what love feels like."
"Thank you for being the brightest part of my youth."
"I carry you. Not as a wound—but as light."
"This is not goodbye. It never was."

""You were the beginning. And because of you, I'm still writing."
? A Final Poem – "Love Doesn't End Here"
Love doesn't end when the voice goes quiet.
Or when the calls stop.
Or when the name fades from others' memories."

Love stays.
In playlists. In sunflowers. In unspoken prayers.
In the way we show up for others,
in the way we heal,
in the way we write.
You left, Smiley.
But love?
Love stayed.
And so did I.
This is where we close the book.
Not with a goodbye—
But with a breath.

And maybe, if you listen close enough—
a quiet smile.
    Thank you for walking through this story.
Through pain. Through poems. Through memory.
    Smiley would've been proud.
And Nani? He's still becoming.
    The end.
But not really.

The Ending Words For All Readers

This isn't the end.
Not really.
    Because healing doesn't come with a final page.
It's not neat. It's not finished.
It's a journey with no straight line—just quiet steps, some forward, some backward, all brave in their own way.
    Writing this book was like holding a mirror to my soul—
seeing all the light, all the shadow,
and learning to love both.
    Smiley will always be a part of me.
Not as a wound, but as a whisper.
Not as pain, but as presence.
    There are still days when her memory breaks me.
But more often now, it builds me.
I smile when I think of her.
And that's how I know I've begun to heal.
    If you've made it to this page,
thank you.
For listening. For feeling.
For walking this road beside me.
    And if you're still in the middle of your own storm—
please remember:
your story doesn't end in the darkness.
There's light waiting for you,
just beyond the next step.
    Choose yourself.
Even when it's hard.
Especially then.

Because sometimes, the softest act of courage
is deciding that you're worth saving.
— Nani